8.99

RNING
TO LEARN
Pocketbook

2nd edition

By Tom Barwood

N

Cartoons:
Hailstone

Published by:

Teachers' Pocketbooks
Laurel House, Station Approach,
Alresford, Hampshire SO24 9JH, UK
Tel: +44 (0)1962 735573
Fax: +44 (0)1962 733637
Email: sales@teacherspocketbooks.co.uk
Website: www.teacherspocketbooks.co.uk

*Teachers' Pocketbooks is an imprint of
Management Pocketbooks Ltd.*

Series editor – Linda Edge.

This edition published 2012. Reprinted 2014.
ISBN: 978 1 906610 51 7

Previous edition published 2005.
ISBN: 978 1 903776 64 3

© Tom Barwood 2005, 2012.

E-book ISBN: 978 1 908284 94 5

British Library Cataloguing-in-Publication
Data – A catalogue record for this book is
available from the British Library.

Design, typesetting and graphics by Efex Ltd.
Printed in UK.

Contents

Introduction

I am fortunate to work in the world's biggest classroom in that I work with hundreds of students every week in schools all over the country and elsewhere. I am also very lucky that I get to teach my best lesson of the week every day of the week.

Working with such large numbers of students from such a diverse geographic and social base has allowed me to understand some universal principles. These are:

1. Regardless of where the school is or what type of background the students come from they are largely motivated (or not) by the same things.
2. There is no such thing as the perfect school – and even if there were, someone on the staff would still find something to complain about!

I always begin my work by asking the students to put their hands up if they know who I am, have met me before or know what I am going to do. Rarely do any hands go up.

DO NOT LOOK IN HERE

Introduction

I then ask them who thinks the course will be boring and normally, without exception, all the hands go up. My next question is, if no one knows me or what I am going to do, how do they know that? Then comes a raft of answers, the most popular being, *'Because it's school'*.

I then ask the students to list all the things they 'can't do'. I normally start with, *'Who can't sing or dance?'* (who would say 'yes' to these things in a public forum?) and then progress through the main subject areas, watching the hands all go up at different but very definite times.

My next question is, *'When did you decide that you couldn't do it'?* Some look puzzled and others simply say, *'I've never been able to do it'*. In response I ask them if they were born like that; did a doctor specifically tell their mothers that there were things they couldn't do?

Introduction

So what do we do with all these students who believe that anything connected with learning has to be **boring** and believe that there is a whole series of things or subjects they just '**can't do**'?

In my view, the only cure for boredom is curiosity. Fortunately there is no cure for curiosity and our task is, therefore, to foster in our students a desire to know more or a thirst to learn.

Similarly, when looking at **can** and **can't do**, we need to develop a belief system in students that says anything is possible – if they want it enough.

The aim of this book is to illustrate in a simple and practical fashion some of the ways we learn. Just like any skill, learning to learn is something you need to keep practising as there is no limit to how far you can take it.

Introduction

This book is designed to be:

- An introduction for teachers to the field known as 'learning to learn'
- A classroom resource to be used by teachers with students
- A resource to be used by students independently
- A guide for parents who want to help their children to learn effectively

Having said this, most of the book is written with a student audience in mind. For this reason I have kept most of the theoretical material (which is likely to be primarily of interest to teachers) in the *Current Thinking* chapter towards the end of the book. A final section lists resources and further reading.

Introduction

Begin by looking through the contents page, familiarising yourself with the chapter headings. Then, flick through the whole book, pausing on pages that catch your eye (this is known as **'skipping'**). Then casually read through the chapters, spending no more than five minutes on a chapter (this is known as **'skimming'**).

This exercise will flag up the areas that are of interest to you and will give you the 'big picture' of what the book is about.

Finally, go back to the areas of real interest for you, read them carefully and try practising a few of the techniques (this is known as **'scouring'**).

You may find it useful to return to particular topics or to re-read topics that you skimmed or skipped before. The book does not set out to be a 'one off' read, as a novel may be, rather it's designed to help throughout the 'learning journey'.

The Big Picture

The power of learning

Many of us assume that learning is something we *should* be able to do, that some people are *good learners* and others *poor learners*. Learning is actually an **active process** that can be learned and applied to a wide variety of situations. Unfortunately, many people don't know what that active process is – or they've never had it explained to them; they just assume they are poor learners.

Other people believe themselves to be good learners, but in fact they've developed a range of quite inefficient methods for learning which they can either apply only in a limited number of circumstances or which are harder work than they should be.

Either way, there is always the potential to improve your learning power.

Your passport to success

Learning to learn is a skill for life. It is not something you need for school that becomes redundant when you leave. In a world of accelerated change and progress the ability to keep on learning, unlearning and relearning is vital for you to be successful.

The ability to learn is probably the most powerful visa you can have stamped in any 'passport to success'.

Being a good learner gives you the ability to deal creatively with any challenge that comes your way and the freedom to pursue any area of interest in your life. By contrast, not being able to learn leaves you stuck, frustrated and powerless. So whether you want to pass an exam, program a computer, sing a song or build a boat then read on.

The how and the why

If you want to learn anything, then you need to be clear about two things:

1. **Why** you want to learn it (*desire*).
2. **How** to learn it (*technique*).

If you know **why** and **how**, then it is a sure thing that you will learn it.

If you have no idea **why** you are trying to learn something, then your brain will simply say, *'Why bother?'* and you will find yourself bored and distracted.

If you do not know **how** to learn it (or worse, so far your attempts to learn it have failed), then your brain will say, *'Don't go there; it's no fun'* and you will quickly find something else to do.

So which of the two is more important?

Want to be a millionaire?

For many people the '**why**' is badly affected by the '**how**' because they have been taught a subject in a way that doesn't work for them. Very often, they believe that they simply can't do it, eg *'I'm no good at spelling'*, *'I can't do Maths'*, *'I'm rubbish at French'* or, *'I'm really thick'*. Beliefs like these will more or less destroy your motivation to learn.

Think about some of the 'can't do' statements you make about yourself. Try writing them down. What evidence do you have for them? Write that down. Very often it is because you couldn't do something at primary school and still believe that you can't do it now. I believed that I couldn't do Maths because we were not a Maths family. *What do Maths families look like?*

Now try asking yourself what it would be like if you **could** do it. How much harder would you be prepared to try something if you were offered a million pounds to do it or alternatively if there was a really serious consequence of failure?

The why of learning

To be successful you need to be able to answer three questions:

1. **What** is it that you want?
2. **How much** do you want it?
3. What are you **prepared** to do to get it?

Most people are stuck because they are not sure **what** they want, or sometimes they know what they want but don't want it enough to make them really take the steps required to get it.

How can we change this?

Make the **why** big enough and the **how** will fall into place.

Achieve your dreams!

It is amazing how many people who say that they can't learn, are able to digest *The Highway Code* (not the most exciting book in the world) when they want to pass their driving test and get behind the wheel of a car.

Even those people who have an idea of what they want (sometimes called a dream) often think that they can't get there because they see all kinds of obstacles in the way, eg lack of money, lack of talent, no sense of urgency, or fear of failure.

Personal 'wish list'

The easiest way to kick-start the process of building the **why** is to get back in touch with the things that matter to you or that you have dreamed of doing.

Try writing down on a piece of paper three to five things under the following headings:

- Which countries in the world would you visit if you only had a year left to live?
- What jobs would you try if you could try any job in the world for just one day?
- What things would you try if you knew you couldn't fail (this does not include robbing a bank or buying a lottery ticket)?
- If you won the lottery what would be the first five things you would buy?
- If you had complete control what five things would you do to make the world a better place?

This is your own personal 'wish list'.

What's in it for me?

If you could see how school or learning could give you access to these things, you would be highly motivated to learn. This is because everyone wants to be successful. It is an ingrained part of being human.

However, the brain is a very sensible thing – it does not give you the energy to learn unless it can clearly see 'What's In It For Me' (WIIFM).

Whenever you are asked to do something the brain does a simple calculation. It weighs up how much **risk** or **effort** the task is going to require and what the **pay-off** is going to be. If your brain can't see that the pay-off is bigger than the risk or effort then it will simply say, *'Don't bother'*.

The trick here is to focus on how school can help you achieve at least some of the things on your wish list. If you think school can't help, then try asking careers staff or people doing a thing that you dream of, what it took to get there – you may be surprised.

The pay-off

Despite the word 'pay' in pay-off you will find that money is not what the brain is looking for. The pay-off is normally emotional rather than financial: people play the lottery because they want to win enough money to give them the freedom and power to live life the way they want. **Freedom** and **choice** are the emotional pay-offs.

The thrill of success is something that we would all like to feel. However, the WIIFM model is unfairly slanted to the risk and effort side because it is dominated by **fear**.

Fear of what? Normally the fear of trying something new and failing (or the thought of failing) makes us feel stupid, and feeling stupid is one of our least favourite emotions. We like to remain 'looking good' – especially in front of friends, family and colleagues.

To avoid ever having that feeling we tend to play safe by staying in the zone in which we are comfortable.

The future is unknown...

You may wonder why this model is slanted so powerfully to the negative. Well the pay-off side tends to be derived from the future – which is completely unknown. Unfortunately the risk and effort side often has a treasure chest of clear evidence of how it feels to fail – called your past. Sadly, our brains tend to focus on all the things we did badly in the past and seem to ignore the more positive memories.

As we progress through life we tend to build up a picture of who we think we are, based on all these different successes and failures. Eventually we think we have a very accurate picture of ourselves, which then dictates all the things we think we can and can't do.

Try the short test on the following page.

How successful are you?

Give yourself a score out of ten (where one is lowest and ten is highest) for each of the following:

- How successful you think you have been so far in life
- How clever you think you are*
- How excited you are about your future

Are you surprised how easy you found it to score yourself with no guidelines? Now complete the test:

- For anywhere you didn't score ten out of ten, write down the reason(s).
- Now write down what you could do to deal with each reason to move yourself up by one point

More details as to what constitutes intelligence can be found on pages 121 – 123. You may find what you read there unexpectedly revealing.

Self responsibility

This picture, or set of beliefs, is what makes you, you. The only person responsible for creating this 'self estimate' is you.

As Henry Ford once said:

*'Whether **you** think **you** can or think **you** can't, **you** are probably right.'*

If this seems a bit confusing, it just means that the only person in charge of how far you go is you!

Too often we ask all the wrong people or listen to all the wrong information (ignoring all the good stuff) to form a 'self estimate'. It's a bit like asking your miserable neighbour what he or she thinks your bike is worth but ignoring what the bike shop has to say.

The three areas of learning

Armed with this new knowledge of yourself, you can now progress to looking at **How** to learn. This falls into three neat but overlapping areas.

- **Registering** – how to take information in
- **Retaining** – how to make information stick
- **Recalling** – how to make sure you can recall information when you need it

The following chapters look at each of these in turn. You will quickly see how the areas overlap and realise that techniques from one stage of the learning process can be used in one or both of the others.

Registering

The difficulty with registering

One of the major problems in learning, before you even start to worry about whether or not you have remembered it, is that many of us don't take in information in the first place.

This can be because you are not:

- **Hearing** the information, as a result of the 'background noise' in your head

- **Absorbing** the information, as it is not presented in a way that is suitable for you to digest

This chapter contains ideas about how you can improve your absorption of information.

The problem with listening

Many of us don't even really hear what is being said to us. This is because if you believe *'I can't do the subject'* or *'it is boring'* then these statements will be playing in your head. It can be a bit like trying to listen to what someone is saying when the radio is on loud in the background.

How many times has someone said to you, *'Are you listening to me?'* and you reply *'Yes'* whilst a voice in the back of your head says *'No'?*

The solution to 'radio boring'

So how do you get over the problem?

- Try to switch 'radio boring' off and give the topic a chance
- Help yourself to focus on what the person is saying by taking rough notes of the key points as the person speaks
- Practise believing that you can do the subject – just not yet!

Another idea is to practise some brain gym. **Brain Gym*** is a series of physical exercises designed to energise your brain by pushing it to make connections to different, often under-used areas of the brain.

For example: try touching your forearm to the opposite thigh. If you can do that, carry on touching each forearm in turn to the opposite thigh. See if you can then extend the exercise, touching each elbow to the opposite knee. Carry on doing that and then see if you can also turn your head in the opposite direction to your arms as you do it.

*Brain Gym is a registered trademark of the Educational Kinesiology Foundation / Brain Gym® International

Become more absorbent!

The next problem is trying to absorb large amounts of information all at once. Parents will tell you that if you try and feed a baby too much food too quickly, you may get it back sooner than you realise! Your brain is just the same.

The next few pages contain ideas about ways in which you can restructure information so that your brain absorbs it more easily and effectively. Try the ideas out in different contexts; some may work better for you than others. Most people find a combination of strategies works best.

However, different brains do work differently, so to get the best out of what follows you might first want to find out more about brain dominance by looking at page 120. I will be referring to brain dominance in this section from time to time.

Skimming

Before you start trying to absorb material in depth take time to skim through the information you are trying to learn. So, with a book, for instance:

* Start by **reading** through the chapter headings
* **Flick** through the pages allowing your eye to wander over the text (from left to right and top to bottom of the pages), from front to back
* **Repeat** this process from the back to the front of the book
* Stick five or six **markers** in the sections that seem relevant to you (remember, at this stage only a handful of things will be vital – imagine you are faced with a large buffet of food and you are trying to pick out a tasty plateful)

Slicing

The easiest way to eat a big meal is by slicing it up into bite-size pieces. In the same way, chop up the information you are trying to digest by:

- Taking a big paragraph and **ruling** off and **numbering** it into smaller sections
- **Grouping** similar sections of information together (you could do this by way of 'cut and paste')

Simplifying

A lot of the language we use in learning can be very confusing in its own right. Sometimes there are just too many words for the message to get through. Simplifying allows you to deal with the problem of 'spare' words. You can:

- **Scribble them out** with a pencil
- **Re-write** the text in your own words (use **abbreviations**, for longer words, eg 'devpt' for 'development', 'govt' for 'government')
- Go through and **highlight** just the important words
- Create **bullet point lists** of key ideas

Alternatively, why not turn the information into a **picture or diagram**?
Creating a diagram or picture with no words at all really gets you to think about the concepts. It might help to imagine that your visual representation is to explain the idea to young children.

The problem with absorbing

It can sometimes be difficult to absorb information because when faced with piles of notes, old coursework and textbooks, it is hard to see the 'bigger picture' of how all the parts fit together.

One of the best ways to help you see the connections between all the different pieces of information is to use networked notes, examples of which are shown in the next few pages.

Networked notes

Networked notes are a very powerful way of absorbing information. They are also an extremely useful method for organising and reviewing information and for generating new ideas. The aim is to move away from making notes in a conventional way and to look at ideas from different angles to make them more accessible to your brain. The information is arranged on the page in different ways: not just starting at the top and working down to the bottom as you do with conventional notes.

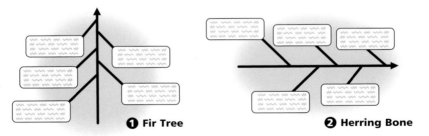

❶ Fir Tree

❷ Herring Bone

Fir Tree and Herring Bone are both good for timelines and processes.

Networked notes

Three other suggestions:

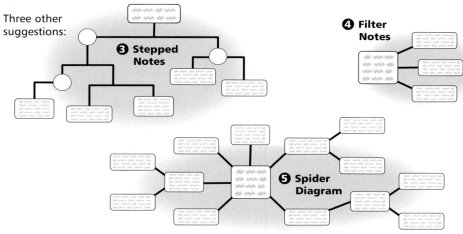

❸ Stepped Notes

❹ Filter Notes

❺ Spider Diagram

Vary your networked notes to suit the task or your way of thinking.
Use different colours for the boxes, links or junctions.

How to Mind Map®*

The most well known method of absorbing information is Mind Mapping, as developed by Tony Buzan. To get you started, here's how to Mind Map:

- Take a large sheet of blank paper, the bigger the better. Turn the paper sideways so that the longer edge is at the bottom (landscape format)
- Find the centre of the paper
- Design an icon or logo that sums up the subject you are studying, eg a globe if it is geography. Put that in the middle of the sheet
- Draw a number of branches coming off that central icon, one for each major topic. Make the branches curved and write the topic names along them. (Imagine that you are doing a Mind Map of your life. What would be the branches? Eg where you live, your hobbies, your family, your pets, etc)

*Mind Map and Mind Mapping are registered trademarks of the Buzan organisation.

How to Mind Map®

- Write only along the branches. (Putting notes at the end of the branches is not Mind Mapping)
- Instead of writing notes at the end of the branches, create pictures that summarise the topic or idea. These should be as fun and colourful as possible
- Each of the branches will then have further sub branches coming off it until you have created a picture which looks as if you are underground staring up at the roots of an enormous tree

It may take you a number of attempts to get this right but, without realising it, you are actually organising and storing the information in your head as you go.

Mind Mapping can also make a great group activity (and if you produce something you are really proud of there is no reason why you can't copy it and make it more widely available – maybe at a price!).

Although the example overleaf is in black and white, Mind Maps work when they are big, colourful and fun to look at.

Personalised Mind Maps

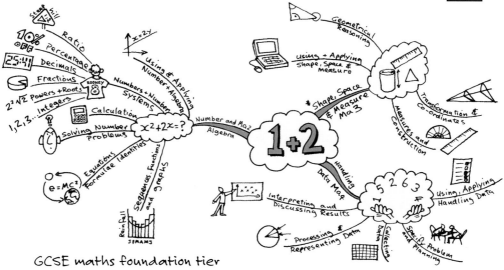

GCSE maths foundation tier

Mind Maps to absorb information

It is not important to be a talented artist to create Mind Maps that will work for you (although if you are they may sell well!). As long as the images you create are personal to you or have particular associations, then the maps you create will do their job.

People sometimes say that only certain types of learners work well with Mind Maps whereas others are better off sticking to the tried and tested formula of linear note-making. In fact, we can all benefit from both, depending on what we are trying to do. Only ever sticking to one method will not produce the best results.

If you really are unconfident about your artwork or want some help in constructing your maps, there is now a wide range of software packages available.

The learning cocktail

Although the ideas here have been presented in sequence, it does not mean that one idea is better than another. Developing your ability to learn is about creating a cocktail of the different techniques that work for you. Each of us will have different ingredients in our cocktail. The only way to find the correct ingredients for yours is to experiment until you find the one that works for you.

Using the senses

One of the most important ingredients of your learning cocktail is using more than just one sense to learn. We have five senses with which to take in information from the outside world – seeing, hearing, tasting, smelling and feeling. Until we invent scratch and sniff notes or edible revision packs, then taste and smell don't play such a big part in learning as the other three.

Most people have a *preferred* sense for absorbing information – mainly **visual**, **auditory** or **kinaesthetic** (ie learning through physically doing/experiencing). You may find that your preferred sense is not the same for every subject. However, if you don't know your preferred sense (sometimes referred to as your 'learning style') and are constantly trying to take information in through a different channel, then you will become frustrated.

Learning styles, and their use in teaching, have come in for some criticism lately – and justifiably so, where the concept has been crudely applied. The obvious thing to bear in mind is that unless we have had our ears bunged up, our eyes poked out or our arms chopped off, then we have to be a **combination of all three styles**.

Learning styles

Broadening the methods you use, both to learn and to teach, will bring unexpected inspiration.

In times of pressure or stress, eg when learning something new or teaching something that people don't seem to be picking up, we tend to default to our preferred sense, entrenching ourselves deeper and deeper in that dominant sense. If the 'deliverer' and 'receiver' are entrenched in different dominant senses, communication is difficult.

If you are unaware of your tendency to retreat into one style or another in times of stress, then you will lack a major resource with which to 'dig yourself out of that hole'.

'If all you have is a hammer, everything looks like a nail'
Abraham Maslow –
psychologist.

Preferred learning style

Working out your preferred learning style is not an exact science. However, many of us do have a definite preference as to the way in which we would rather learn. In fact, our preferred learning style is part of the way we process the world around us.

No one learning style is better than another and the following questionnaire may indicate that none of your learning styles is particularly dominant. However, the results can be a real revelation for some people.

To complete the questionnaire, simply read each question and rate yourself against the three answers by putting 1, 2 and 3 in the white boxes where 1= first choice/most preferred answer, 2 = second choice and 3 = third choice. you may only use each number once in answering each question.

How do you like to learn?

Question	Answers	Score A	B	C
1. When you are being praised for doing something well, which do you prefer?	To receive a written note			
	To hear the praise said to you			
	To be given a pat on the back or a hug			
2. Given a choice, how do you prefer to relax?	Watching TV, video, film or reading a book			
	Listening to music or the radio			
	Playing sport/computer games, or just doing something			
3. If you have something to sort out with someone, which would you rather do?	Talk with the person face-to-face			
	Discuss it with the person on the 'phone			
	Discuss it whilst doing something else, eg walking			

How do you like to learn?

Question	Answers	Score		
		A	B	C
4. **Which phrase best describes you?**	I talk quickly and sometimes don't listen to others			
	I enjoy listening to others but am keen to talk			
	I talk slowly and use lots of hand movements			
5. **When you remember someone or something, what do you do?**	Remember the face first then the name			
	Remember the name first and then the face			
	Remember where/when you met them and what you did			
6. **If you are lost or need to get somewhere, what helps most?**	A map			
	Someone telling you the way			
	Someone showing you the way			

How do you like to learn?

Question	Answers	Score A	B	C
7. When you are spelling a difficult word, what do you do?	See the word			
	Spell the word out loud			
	Write the word down to see if it feels right			
8. When you are angry with someone, what do you do?	Go quiet and fume inside			
	Tell the person exactly what you think			
	Storm off, slamming doors			
9. When you are trying to concentrate, what distracts you most?	Untidiness			
	Noise			
	Movement			
Add up the numbers in each column	Totals			

Learning style questionnaire – results

The three totals should add up to 54. If they don't, check your scores. Those with:

- **A** as the lowest score may have a preference for **visual learning**
- **B** as the lowest score may have a preference for **auditory learning**
- **C** as the lowest score may have a preference for **Kinaesthetic** or **physical learning**

Whilst most of us have a **preference** as to learning style, the best way for everybody to learn is by using all three senses. Even if you have a dominant sense, this doesn't mean that you are unable to learn using the other two senses.

Remember too, that it is your responsibility to find ways of interpreting information into your style. Your preferred learning style cannot be used as an excuse for failing to learn. The next few pages give some examples of how to use the three different learning styles.

Visual learning

For visual learning, try these techniques:

- Write down the key facts, creating **key facts cards**. You can then lay them out in front of yourself

- Aim to 'visualise' what you are learning. Sit back, look up and try to **see a picture** of the ideas or information. Eg if you are trying to remember one of Stalin's five-year plans, see him sitting at his desk with each of the elements of the plan laid out in front of him including model farms, factories and hospitals

- Write important facts on Post-it® notes and **stick them in strategic places**! Eg the bathroom mirror, your wardrobe, your bedside table

- Use **mind maps, pictures, cartoon story boards, photo stories and diagrams** to summarise information

Visual learning

- Put the information into a **screenplay** of a favourite film or TV soap, comedy or sitcom, using your favourite characters
- **Watch** relevant TV programmes, films, DVDs, Internet video clips
- Go to the library or bookshop and search for **illustrated books** with a lot of pictures (ones aimed at small children can often demystify a topic or give you a good overview. Don't be shy!)

Auditory learning

For auditory learning, try these techniques:

- Summarise the subject **in your own words**
- **Read your notes out loud** as you go through them, perhaps in strange voices
- Sit back, look from side to side and mentally rehearse delivering your notes as a **speech** on the stage (to a very important audience where you are definitely the star turn)
- Make audio tapes or CDs of the information and **play them back** to yourself (especially just before you go to sleep)
- **Explain the subject to other people** (especially if they have never come across it before and you have to go back to basics in your explanation)

Auditory learning

- If possible, find other ways of having the subject explained to you, for example relevant **radio and TV programmes, talks, lectures,** going to the **cinema or theatre**

- Turn the information into **song lyrics, rhymes or raps** of your own and practise playing them over and over inside your head

- Put a famous tune to the information and **sing it** back to yourself

Kinaesthetic learning

For Kinaesthetic learning, try these techniques:

- **Move about** as you learn. If you can't leave your desk whilst at school, then use your hands and arms, eg doing the nine times table on your fingers. (If you have never heard of this trick, your mission is to find someone who can teach it to you and then you must teach it to someone else. (Try your maths teacher as a starting point)

- **Use actions** to imprint the information on your body, eg when completing multiplication sums, make a cross with your hands and develop other gestures to represent the other elements of the sum. You are tapping out the sums on parts of your body

- **Use actions** for different ideas, eg when memorising the gender of objects in French, **clap** once for a masculine noun, clap twice for a feminine noun and **click** your left fingers and then your right fingers for the plural

Kinaesthetic learning

- **Retype** the information on a computer into a colour, font and print size that appeals to you
- Write down the key facts, creating key facts cards. You can then **shuffle** them like a pack of cards and keep reading them
- Give yourself **'kinaesthetic breaks'**, eg juggling, knitting, practising the drums (even without a drum kit this works)
- **Make models** representing the information, eg use Lego, clay, straws, pipe-cleaners or sand paper (great for remembering abrasion, in river erosion). Use toy figures (or anything suitable representing them) to plot the movements of countries and armies in World War I
- Create **big, bold mind maps** that allow you to express the information freely

That perfect cocktail

If you have a clear dominance in one sense then it is logical to start with that sense, eg making notes, reading out loud or using actions and then 'hammer it home' with the other two senses.

If you have a less obvious dominance then you may wish to start with a multi-sensory approach, eg start by reading the information off the page out loud, whilst walking around the room. Not only will this be more effective than just using one learning style, but it will also be a lot more fun and will prevent your learning from becoming tedious.

As a predominantly visual learner, who has a lot of information to absorb on a regular basis, I always:

- Start by reading the information and making notes (including using mind maps)
- Then try to repeat the information back to myself without looking at the text or the notes
- Go for a run and repeatedly mumble the information back to myself (quietly!)

Remember: Developing *your* ability to learn is about creating that perfect cocktail.

The Big Picture

 Registering

 Retaining ◀

 Recalling

 Healthy Mind

 Current Thinking

 Further Information

Retaining

Magic memory

Memory is one of our most important brain functions. Without it we would be lost. However, many of us are let down by what we believe to be a poor memory. There are three things you should bear in mind:

- It is accessing your memory, not a lack of it, that can be the problem
- A good memory is not innate – just like a muscle it gets stronger with use
- Having a good memory is a result of using proven techniques

It is also worth remembering that a good memory has been seen to be a better indicator of success in exams than a high IQ. It is worth developing that muscle!

The problem with memory

The dividing line between registering and retaining information is not as precise as the chapter headings in this book might suggest: ie if you have already started to use the VAK techniques (pages 46 to 52) to **register** information in the section on learning styles, then you will automatically **retain** more of that information.

There are certain things that you are aware have been imprinted into your memory without you even trying, eg your first day at secondary school, what you were doing on Christmas Day, or the day you learned to ride a bike. These are all very personal and outstanding images as they were important days in your life.

The question is: how can you use the same memory capacity for things that you don't find quite as momentous, interesting or exciting (eg revision!)?

Developing a mega memory

You might like to take some advice from the world memory champions:

- You have to have the motivation to want to do it
- All memory is a result of visual association
- Use the POA technique – Person, Object, Action. First, turn the thing you are trying to remember into a person. Then get that person to be doing something on or with an object. You can now link each of the people and actions into a longer story or by placing them into a familiar journey (see page 68). This can be done with words and numbers. The more extreme the images and the actions the more likely you are to remember them.

Pages 60 – 74 explain in greater detail some of the other techniques. You don't have to use all of them, or use them in the order in which they are presented, to be successful.

The seven keys

We all have phenomenal memories (in fact, sometimes it would be helpful if we could forget a few incidents along the way!). Scientists tell us that we naturally remember certain things above others – these are 'the seven keys' to memory, as follows:

- Outstanding
- Funny
- Personal
- Emotional
- Linked to our senses
- Connected with sex
- The first and last thing we learn (in a lesson or revision session, for instance)

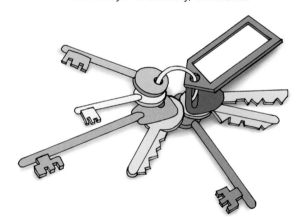

Using the keys

If what you are trying to learn is not one of these seven keys then it is highly unlikely that you will remember it so ensure that your registering techniques make use of the seven keys. For example:

- When creating a mind map, make sure that it is outstanding by making it really bright and colourful
- When repeating information back to yourself, use crazy voices and witty rhymes
- Design actions that are imaginative and distinctive (don't hold back, no one's watching!)

Memory techniques

The following pages describe the most popular effective techniques for memorising information. Try them out to see which ones work for you:

1. Mnemonics.
2. Mind pegs.
3. Reports, films and journeys.
4. Using your body.
5. Using consistent images.
6. Patterns, prices and tunes.
7. Numbers and images.

Mnemonics

Mnemonics work by turning the first letter of a list of items (or the letters of a word which is difficult to spell) into a memorable sentence or word.

You might remember some of these from primary school:

- The word 'because' = **b**ig **e**lephants **c**an **a**lways **u**pset **s**mall **e**lephants
- The colours of the rainbow = **R**ichard **o**f **Y**ork **g**ave **b**attle **i**n **v**ain
  (red, orange, yellow, green, blue, indigo, violet)
- The points of the compass = **n**ever **e**at **s**hredded **w**heat or **n**aughty **e**lephants **s**quirt **w**ater
  (north, east, south, west)
- The Great Lakes of North America = HOMES
  (Huron, Ontario, Michigan, Erie and Superior).

Creating mnemonics that work

Somehow the older we get the less likely we are to use mnemonics, despite the fact that we still remember (and often use) the ones we learned all that time ago. The problem is that sometimes the mnemonics we make up ourselves don't work.

They may not work for a number of reasons:

1. **The sentence doesn't flow**. I have heard many mnemonics for memorising trigonometry, for instance. None of them worked for me except:
   - **S**ex **O**n **H**oliday (sine = opposite/hypotenuse)
   - **C**an **A**lways **H**elp (cosine = adjacent/hypotenuse)
   - **T**he **O**ld **A**ged (tan = opposite/adjacent)

Creating mnemonics that work

2. **They don't involve the seven keys to memory** (page 57). For example, you may require a mnemonic to be funny to be memorable. The mnemonic on the previous page works especially well for me when I imagine my own granny saying this phrase to me after she has just been arrested for chasing Robbie Williams down Yarmouth seafront on the annual Women's Institute day out.

3. **You can remember the mnemonic but not what it is supposed to tell you.** Lots of people know the mnemonic for the nine planets of the solar system (My Very Easy Method Just Speeds Up Naming Planets) but either get the planets in the wrong order or can't remember them. Some suggested ways round this problem are listed on the next pages.

Mnemonics – stories and lists

Create a story
In the case of the planets you might see a picture of Freddy **Mercury** walking into Planet Hollywood leading **Venus** Williams by the hand and Michael Jackson is on stage singing the **Earth** song whilst trying to eat a **Mars** bar. His hair catches fire and Fireman Sam turns up in his fire engine, **Jupiter**…Try finishing the story off yourself.

Attach songs or lines from songs to the objects in a list.
For example, Pluto – 'Who let the dogs out?' (Will Smith); Venus – 'I'm your Venus, I'm your fire, your desire' (Bananarama). (If you want to hear the most amazing musical performance of the whole periodic table, then go to www.privatehand.com/flash/elements.html.)

Mnemonics – get moving!

Add movement to your mnemonic
To spell the word 'rhythm' put your hands on
your hips, and chant '**R**hythm **H**as **Y**our **T**wo
Hips **M**oving' whilst swinging your hips from
side to side.

You don't have to invent all your own
mnemonics. Ask as many people as you can
for their favourites and write them all down in
one place. Maybe you could produce a school
booklet of mnemonics for each subject, made
up with contributions from staff members,
students and parents.

Mind pegs – step one

Some people find memorising lists or strings of information difficult as they can't think of a story. That need not be a problem – you can borrow some 'off the peg' stories or ideas. The Bun, Shoe, Tree method is perhaps the best known example.

In this system each of the numbers between one and ten has an image that goes with it:

One – Bun

Two – Shoe

Three – Tree

Four – Door

Five – Hive

Six – Sticks

Seven – Heaven

Eight – Gate

Nine – Wine

Ten – Hen

The **first** job is to memorise the sequence above.

Mind pegs – step two

Second, take the list you are trying to learn and attach each item from that list to an image from the sequence. In doing this, make the connections between the images and items on the list personal to you.

Example Take the list of the seven things that all living creatures do (eat, move, reproduce, excrete, sense, breathe, grow). This is the order I have put them in; your order might be different if the connections work differently for you. Now pair off the sequence and your arrangement of the list of items, eg:

1. Bun   – Eat
2. Shoe   – Move
3. Tree   – Reproduce
4. Door   – Excrete
5. Hive   – Sense
6. Sticks – Breathe
7. Heaven – Grow

Mind pegs – step three

Now attach an image to each pair eg:

1. Bun – Eat – imagine an elephant eating a sticky bun from your bag
2. Shoe – Move – look at the elephant and realise it is wearing running shoes
3. Tree – Reproduce – imagine a pair of love birds in a tree
4. Door – Excrete – imagine someone banging on the toilet door demanding to be let in.

Try finishing the sequence.

Once you have a series of images you can run them together into one story.

A great place to practise this technique is going shopping eg if you have three things to buy, remember Bun, Shoe, Tree and connect them with the images of what you have to buy.

Reports, films and journeys

There are yet more ways of retaining information which may suit you:

- Describe the story as a police report (begin with *'Well, your Honour...'*); or as a story you are telling to small children (begin with *'Once upon a time...'*); or see it as if you are filming it with a camera and then watching it on a screen (begin with *'Lights, cameras, action...'*)

- Imagine a journey that you regularly take eg the walk to school, a trip round the supermarket or your way into town. 'Paste' the images of what you have to remember into that journey. This works especially well if you create the situations using the seven keys (see page 57)

  You may wish to practise this as a class, memorising images 'pasted' around the school corridors (you may even want to walk the route first).

Use your body

Another way of retaining information is to number off **parts of your body**: top of your head, mouth, end of your nose, shoulders, hands and so on until you get down to your feet and then imagine each object from the list sitting on one of the parts of the body

Scientists tell us that the conscious brain can hold up to seven pieces of information at a time plus or minus two. Therefore, the worst you will ever do is to remember five pieces. So, memorise information in **blocks of five** things.

Use consistent images

This strategy works with foreign languages. If you are trying to remember
which words are masculine and which feminine then attach a feminine or masculine
image to each one that will always remind you. For example, for me:

- All feminine words are always associated with long diamond earrings and I create
  an image reflecting that, eg la **bougie** = candle: visualise a **budgie** in a cage
  nibbling on a candle and wearing long diamond earrings
- All masculine words somehow involve a pipe eg le **trottoir** = pavement: visualise
  the **Trotter** family (Del Boy, Rodney etc.) driving their three-wheeler up the
  pavement with big pipes in their mouths

Could you think of examples for doing this in German? Eg could every masculine
noun (where 'the' is 'der') involve Homer Simpson?

Patterns and prices

We are not designed to remember strings of numbers unless they have some special significance, eg if I told you next week's winning lottery numbers or perhaps the phone number of someone you would really like to speak to (!) you would find a way of remembering them. But as always, there are some solutions:

- Look for **associations, patterns or rhythms** in the sequence, eg I find it hard to remember my in-laws' wedding date as 8 August 1964 but I do know that 8 x 8 = 64 (08/08/64)

- It helps to '**chunk**' the sequence into blocks that you find memorable. Many people find blocks of two digits easy to recall. Maybe that is why French telephone numbers are always written in pairs of digits

- Remember a number as a **price**, eg a four digit PIN (4560) for the bank could be expressed as £45.60

- Put **a tune** to the string of numbers. Double glazing adverts on the radio often use this technique to great effect

Numbers and images – step one

Create images that look like the numbers, eg:

1 = a pen

2 = a swan

3 = a bumble bee

4 = a sailing boat

5 = ...

6 = ...

7 = ...

8 = ...

9 = ...

10 = ...

Finish off the sequence up to 10 yourself.

Numbers and images – step two

Now use these images in a story so that you remember them in sequence.
For example:

Battle of Waterloo in 1815:
1 = pen,   8 = fat lady,   1 = pen,   5 = a big hook.

Imagine a giant fountain pen with a large opera singer
standing on top of it, using a second giant fountain
pen to balance with, whilst being suspended by a
hook from a crane. You might wish to reverse the
image (with the hook at the bottom) to make it
work for you.

You could also use the Bun, Shoe, Tree method
(pages 65–67) to remember dates:

Battle of Hastings in 1066:
Hen, Sticks, Sticks – so imagine a chicken holding
chopsticks under its wings.

Numbers and poems

You can use words to remember numbers too. To remember Pi, count the number of letters in each word of the following poem and write them down in the same order. Insert a decimal point after the first digit and you will have the value of Pi to 20 decimal places:
3.14159265358979323846

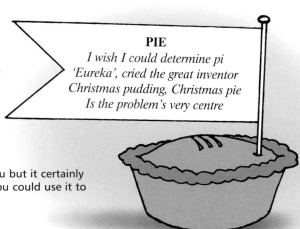

PIE

I wish I could determine pi
'Eureka', cried the great inventor
Christmas pudding, Christmas pie
Is the problem's very centre

This may be of no use to you but it certainly proves the technique and you could use it to impress your friends!

The problem of 'memory fade'

In many cases, people feel confident they have absorbed and retained the information only to find after a few days that the memory has faded or disappeared completely when it is most needed, eg in an exam or when you are under pressure to remember it.

Why does this happen?

- Information **fades** because of what is called the Ebbinghaus memory decay curve. You can see this from the graph on the next page

  It is not always as dramatic a curve as that shown in the graph but something close to it is happening for all of us, especially when we learn new information.

  If up to 80% of the information is gone by the next day, your brain will ask 'why bother revising?'

'Memory fade' – the graph

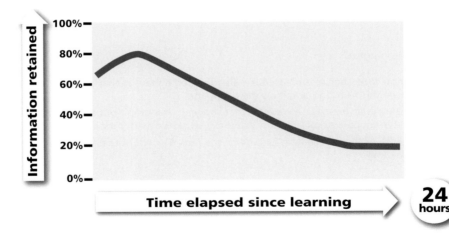

'Memory fade' – the solution

The solution to memory fade is to **review** the information.

'All learning without reviewing is like trying to fill the bath with the plug out'
Mike Hughes –
Closing the Learning Gap.

No matter how big you think the 'bath' is or how fast you think you can turn the 'taps' on, the information is always leaking away.

Reviewing

So how do you **review** information? You do **not** simply try relearning it.

The next four pages offer four different techniques you can use to **review** information and improve **recall**:

- Transforming
- Verbalising
- Reducing
- Snowballing

Transforming

Transforming is the process of turning existing material into something else. To do this, your brain has to really focus on the material and by doing so will retain more of it.

One way of transforming information is to force yourself to use a different sense from the one you would naturally use to remember or communicate the idea, eg try explaining to someone how to tie shoelaces whilst sitting on your hands. You will find this difficult because tying shoelaces is a naturally kinaesthetic activity and you now have to rely on your auditory and visual senses (and therefore have to think about it more carefully).

Two other effective methods of transforming information are **verbalising** it and **reducing** it. Examples are given on the next two pages.

Verbalising

One of the best ways to glue the information into your brain is to **describe it to somebody else**. In doing this you force your brain to make connections in all kinds of new ways.

The best audience is someone who knows nothing of the subject you are talking about. You have to try harder to help them understand and in doing so you make it clearer to yourself. Small children can fit this bill, but as I found with my nieces and nephews, they tire of the 'game' very quickly! So I practise teaching the idea to an imaginary class of primary school children.

The more people you explain the information to the better. If there really is no one around, then describe what you have been learning to the cat or your pet hamster.

This technique is powerful because it has been estimated that we take in 10% of what we see, 20% of what we hear, 50% of what we see and hear and an amazing 95% of what we teach someone else.

Reducing

Another fun way of **reviewing** is to set yourself crazy time limits in which to complete the task, eg can you:

- Retell the basic plot of Macbeth in less than one minute?
- List the verbs that take *être* in the past tense in fifteen seconds?
- List and describe the four processes of coastal erosion in ninety seconds?

There are three ways of timing yourself:

- Use an egg timer (or the stopwatch on your mobile phone)
- Ask your revision buddy to time you (see page 91)
- complete the task during one track of your favourite CD (approximately 2–3 minutes)

These strategies also help you get used to the idea of working to the clock which you need to do for your exams.

Snowballing

A final reviewing technique is to write down **individual words** you can remember from what you have learned rather than whole chunks of information.

This exercise can work really well in pairs or larger groups. You choose a topic and take it in turns to say two words that you remember from the topic until all of you have run out of ideas. This makes a great 'knock out' competition.

It's called 'snowballing' because you start with just two words and keep rolling the ball, sticking new words to it so that it gets larger and larger. It works because single words are much easier to remember than long sentences and building up the knowledge in stages is:

- Less threatening
- More fun
- Quietly effective (the words will carry a string of information with them in your head)

Which method works best?

Much like the other techniques discussed in this book, when it comes to reviewing, your own combination of the available methods will have the best results.

However, to firmly fix the plug into the bath of learning you need to **review** what you have learned at specific intervals.

Intervals

Reviewing information that you have already worked on before means you are not 'starting from scratch'. The process is rather like taking two steps forward and one step back. Even though you won't remember everything from last time, you will be building on existing knowledge.

The technique works most powerfully when you **review** what you have learned at the following intervals from the time that you first learned it:

- 30 minutes
- 24 hours
- One week
- One month, etc

The more often you review information the longer it will stick and the less it will fade.

Be careful what you review!

The Big Picture

 Registering

 Retaining

 Recalling

 Healthy Mind

 Current Thinking

 Further Information

Recalling

Unlocking your memory

We have **registered** the information (ie made sure that it has gone in);
retained it (ie neatly stored it away); now we need to make sure that we can **recall** it
(ie it can be retrieved) when we need it, often when we are under pressure.

The reason you sometimes cannot recall what you know you have properly **registered**
and **retained** is that you are stressed. We all need a certain level of stress to get us
going, but what is one person's challenge can be another person's stress.

What you are trying to prevent happening is your brain 'shutting down' and going
into 'fight, flight, flock or freeze' mode. This is its natural survival reaction to
threatening situations (remember, thinking you are going to fail an exam is one of the
most threatening situations you will come across).

Stress-busting

There are a number of ways you can manage stress both leading up to and
during your exams (or other times of pressure). These include:

- Sleep, diet and exercise (see pages 99–102)
- Practising self-belief techniques
- Relaxation techniques (including meditation and breathing techniques)
- Visualising (focusing on mental images of success)
- Tricks of the trade (finding out from successful people how they did it)
- Preparation and planning (see next few pages)

There are many books and sources of information available on these topics and the
part they can play in exam technique. If in doubt, ask for help.

Be prepared

The most powerful way of making sure your performance does not suffer as a result of stress is to be adequately prepared. The best way to make sure that you are adequately prepared (and believe it) is to know that you have revised effectively.

Many people do not know how to revise effectively. Instead, they spend hours sitting by themselves imagining that they are revising, somehow hoping that if they stare at the book for long enough, the information will eventually go in. Others believe that they can perform an act of magic on the day and, therefore, don't bother revising at all.

Effective revision requires structure.

Early bird or night owl?

First, use the questionnaire that follows to determine whether you're an early bird or a night owl. We all have different ways of working and trying to work outside those times will not be productive for you.

- Read each question
- Enter the letter of the answer which best suits you in the Result column

Question	Answers	Result
1. When your alarm goes off, what do you do?	a) Get straight out of bed b) Switch off the alarm and get up slowly c) Put the alarm onto 'snooze' d) Switch off the alarm and go back to sleep	
2. What time do you go to bed on Sunday nights?	a) 8 – 9pm b) 9 – 10pm c) 10 –11pm d) After 11pm	
3. What time do you get up on Saturday mornings?	a) Before 9am b) 9 – 10am c) 10 – 11am d) After 11am	

Early bird or night owl?

Question	Answers	Result
4. How hungry are you at breakfast time?	a) Very hungry b) Slightly hungry c) Not really hungry d) Disgusted by the thought of food	
5. At what time of day do you feel most lively?	a) Morning b) Afternoon c) Evening d) Late at night	
6. How quickly do you fall asleep?	a) In ten minutes b) 10 – 20 minutes c) 20 – 30 minutes d) More than 30 minutes	

Now score as follows: a = 4, b = 3, c = 2, d = 1

If you score:

6 – 11 points: You're a night owl and will work better towards the end of the day

12 – 18 points: You're neither a night owl nor an early bird and so can be flexible as to your best learning times

19 – 24 points: You are an early bird and will work better at the beginning of the day

Structure and preparation

If it suits the way you learn, find people with similar working times to you and form a revision group with them. Agree times when you'll work and what you'll cover.

Next:

- Decorate your working area with images of success, eg the things you dream of having or doing, or a mock certificate of the grades you'd love to get. This will focus your mind on why you are revising
- Organise your working area so that it does not interfere with absorbing information. Few people work better on a messy desk!
- Make sure you have to hand all the tools you need to revise, eg pens, pencils, highlighter pens, Post-its®, rough paper
- Gather up all your relevant exercise books and files and read through them. If things are missing, get replacements. Use markers to indicate the main sections
- Create a mind map of what has to be done

Time plans

Now you need to **sort out a time plan**. Three things are important to remember at this stage:

1. The human brain works best for **one and a half hours at a time**.
2. You can focus in a concentrated fashion for periods of about **20 to 25 minutes**.
3. You remain much more focused if you have a reward waiting for you at the end of the work. This is called the **Test/Reward model** and is unlike the Reward/Test model used by most people, eg '*I will start my homework after I have eaten my tea*'. You should be working first and then having a reward.

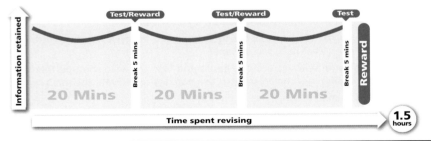

Creating a time plan

Some people spend more time writing their time plans than actually putting them into practice. One of the best ways to revise is just to begin. Do 20 minutes, see how you got on and start building up your plan from there. Remember: 'Ready, Fire, Aim'!

Also, life is dynamic. To believe you can have a perfect plan from which you will never deviate is ridiculous – if you get an irresistible invitation, then go, but make sure you have a catch-up plan in place.

However, beware of the evil demon called *'I'll just...'*. If I had a penny for every time I have sat down to work and thought *'I'll just check my e-mails'* and then found myself still happily distracted by them two hours later, I would be a very rich man! Work your plan and plan your work!

There is neither a perfect revision plan nor the perfect time and place to work. You don't always have to be at home, at a desk or working between the hours of nine and five to revise effectively.

Filling in your time plan

The best goals in life are DIM (Demanding, Imaginative, Moveable).

Therefore, always start with a rough plan of the general shape of your revision dictated by which exams come first. Then:

- Create a blank sheet for each week as per the example on page 96
- Fill it in using pencil so that it can be rubbed out and amended (or the electronic equivalent)
- Give it some shape by putting in all the 'structural points' of your week, eg mealtimes, favourite TV programmes, social commitments, etc. These are your 'rewards'
- Fit your learning around the rewards to conform to the 'test/reward' model. Work in 'test blocks' of ninety minutes. Strange though it may seem, if you have a dentist appointment at 11.00, that can be your reward – and 90 minutes prior to it is your 'test' time

Filling in your time plan

- Within the 90 minute slots make sure that you work in bursts of 20 to 25 minutes
- At the end of each burst, test yourself and take a 'mini-break' for four or five minutes
- You can have as many test blocks in a day as you wish, but try and make sure that you do something completely different in between each block
- You may also find that you work better at certain times of the day, so plan your test blocks accordingly
- Use the **registering** methods described in pages 28 to 30 when you are working and the **retaining** methods described in pages 59 to 74 when you are testing your knowledge

If your days and week lack basic structure, then ring people up and create some. Offer to walk the neighbour's dog or do a job around the house.

Time planner blank

	6.00 am	7.00	8.00	9.00	10.00	11.00	12.00	1.00 pm	2.00	3.00	4.00	5.00	6.00	7.00	8.00	9.00	10.00	11.00 pm	12.00
Mon																			
Tues																			
Wed																			
Thur																			
Fri																			
Sat																			
Sun																			

Get into the habit of **sharing** your plans and allowing others to help keep you on track. **Tick off** tasks when you have completed them, **congratulate** yourself on having done them and **look forward** to sticking it all in the bin when you have finished.

The Big Picture

 Registering

 Retaining

 Recalling

 Healthy Mind ◀

 Current Thinking

 Further Information

Healthy Mind

The basics

The following things are vital for effective learning:

- Sleep
- Switching off
- Food, drink, oxygen
- Positive beliefs

It is surprising how much difference can be made to your learning ability by getting these things right.

Why make things more difficult for yourself than you need to?

Sleep

The right quantity of good quality sleep is essential to being able to learn.

Tiredness caused by going to bed too late is easy to remedy. Just turn the TV off and go to bed! If you don't feel tired, just go to bed anyway.

For most teenagers and adults, an average of eight hours' sleep is normally enough and a lot more (or less) than that can be detrimental.

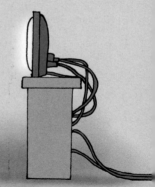

Switching off

If you are going to bed at the right times but wake up tired then you are possibly stressed. Practising **relaxation techniques** can really help. One of the easiest is the 'Seven Eleven' breathing method. Practise breathing in to a count of seven and out to a count of eleven.

Similarly, listening to **relaxation and visualisation CDs** can help enormously.

Do not work too late into the evening – take time to switch off before you go to bed. However, quickly reviewing what you have learned just before you go to sleep can have a very powerful effect on retaining it.

Treating your exams as the only thing in your life and believing that the results (or lack of them) are going to ruin or affect your whole life (forever) is not helpful. **Keep things in perspective** and make sure that you take time out to do what you enjoy.

Food and drink

Obviously, without food, drink and oxygen you would not last very long.
However, the right types of food and drink and levels of oxygen will vastly improve the performance of your brain.

Imagine your brain's a fantastic sports car – would you fill the tank with cheap fuel?

Fruit, salads and oily fish (sardines, tuna, mackerel etc) will do far more to boost your brainpower than sweet, sugary foods (although the occasional treat can help).

Sky juice, council champagne – call it what you like, but **water** helps the brain to function. Tea, coffee, and sugary, caffeine-filled fizzy drinks are nice but they actually have the opposite effect. Try to restrict your intake of these.

Enough oxygen

The brain only weighs approximately three pounds, but it takes 25% of your blood and oxygen requirement. **Sit still too long and your brain starts to switch off**. Just by standing up you increase the blood flow to the brain by 15%.

Exercise oxygenates the system – so, walk the dog, cycle, skip, swim, play a sport, start running, work out, dig the garden or help with the housework. It doesn't matter what you do as long as it gets your heart rate up.

Brain Gym can be particularly effective in keeping your brain energised.
(See page 113 for more information.)

Belief

Remember Henry Ford on page 21? Listen to what you say to people: are you positive about yourself or do you constantly run yourself down? It is not about becoming a big-head or bragging, but if you tell people often enough that you think you're not very good at something, your brain will start to believe it and perform to suit.

Keep words like 'but', 'never', 'can't', 'should', 'must' and 'impossible' out of your vocabulary; use words such as 'hope', 'might', 'can', 'will' and 'do' instead.

Visualise pictures of yourself being successful. Top athletes practise seeing positive pictures of themselves powering over the finishing line, winning the race and receiving their winners' medals. They do not focus on failure.

Belief

Don't spend your life comparing yourself with other people. You will always find people who are better or worse at things than you. Be clear about what you enjoy and what you want for your life and keep telling yourself, '*I can*'.

A healthy mind is heavily dependent upon a healthy body – so don't overlook one in your quest for the other!

The Big Picture

Registering

Retaining

Recalling

Healthy Mind

Current Thinking ◀

Further Information

Current Thinking

Sources of inspiration

As a full-time classroom teacher I often felt that I lived in two caves connected by a tunnel (especially in the winter when I would get up in the dark and go home in the dark). I had the marking cave (home) connected by the long tunnel called 'the drive to work' to the teaching cave (school). Each cave seemed short of light and inspiration due to workload and lack of contact with other adults.

Travelling round the country, I now meet many teachers who feel the same and yet we all have an abundance of good ideas and great materials we've picked up along the way – if only we had the time and opportunity to share them. What I have tried to do in this section is to share some of what I have picked up in a short summary of current thinking, identifying some of the authors and ideas that are shaping education today. You might find these pages flag areas of interest to follow up in more detail; they offer a guide to some of the titles listed in the further information section.

The teaching and learning process

Some schools start from the premise that there's no point in exploring all the theories 'out there' until you can get the students to sit down and listen, and that **behaviour management** should be the focus. However, in schools that *have* concentrated on developing **teaching and learning**, behaviour tends to be positively affected too.

In reality, learning to learn techniques work best where behaviour management strategies are being implemented **at the same time**. This 'combination approach' is reflected in current thinking which has evolved enormously in the last 15 years. It is around 40 years since Colin Rose coined the phrase 'accelerated learning', now a mainstream concept that underpins much of what happens in 21st century classrooms.

As Mike Hughes, education author and trainer, suggests, there are three things that affect the teaching and learning process – **state**, **style** and **structure**.

Structure and style

Looking at these three areas in reverse order, the approach to the **structure** of lessons has evolved under the key stage 3 national strategy. Perhaps influential were Alistair Smith's Seven Stage Lesson Plan (from *Accelerated Learning in Practice* and *Accelerated Learning in the Classroom*) and Mike Hughes' Four Stage Lesson Plan (from *Strategies for Closing the Learning Gap* and *Tweak to Transform*).

A great deal of the work done to date has been on the **style in which we teach**. This uses some of the basic principles of neuro-linguistic programming (NLP) developed by Richard Bandler and John Grinder (see *Introducing NLP* by O'Connor and Seymour and *Righting the Educational Conveyor Belt* by John Grinder).

A key principle is the idea that people can be divided into broad categories dependent upon their 'representational system' (visual, auditory or kinaesthetic). These systems not only affect body language, speech patterns, motivation and breathing but also the way in which we prefer to learn.

NLP

NLP has spawned an array of theories, some based on only one strand of what can seem a complex body of knowledge. For example, Shelle Rose Charvet has refined the NLP concept of 'meta-programs' (the filter systems each person uses to make sense of the world) in *Words that Change Minds*. She uses meta-programs in language to effect motivation.

One of the earliest methods adopted from the world of NLP was of teaching children differently based upon their preferred learning styles (see Eric Jensen's *Super Teaching* and Gordon Dryden and Jeanette Vos' *The Learning Revolution*).

Unfortunately, this led to 'pigeon-holing' students into one category or another and unsubtle attempts to ensure that there was one part of the lesson for each type of learner. This is insufficient and does little to address the bias introduced by the teacher's preferred style.

Learning style

Barbara Prashnig, in her book *Power of Diversity*, and Paul Ginnis, in his *Teachers' Toolkit*, develop the 'learning styles concept' to a much more sophisticated level. In particular, Prashnig's 'working styles analysis' recommends an 'atomised' approach, ie a teaching style tailored to each individual student.

In *Using Your Learning Styles* Peter Honey and Alan Mumford divide learners amongst four categories:
- Activist: 'hands on learner'
- Reflector: 'tell me learner'
- Theorist: 'convince me learner'
- Pragmatist: 'show me learner'

Howard Gardner's concept of 'multiple intelligence' (explained in David Lazear's *Seven Pathways of Learning: Teaching Students and Parents about Multiple Intelligences*) has been used in a variety of ways to create different methods of learning within a classroom experience.

Science

Confusion has sometimes been caused through not making sufficiently clear the difference between **intelligence type** and preferred **learning style**. **Intelligence types** are 'broad avenues' down which learners may access different subjects; in contrast **learning styles** are the ways students prefer to process the information within that avenue. A good example of an approach which combines learning style, intelligence type and hemisphere dominance is described on page 70 of Mike Hughes' *Tweak to Transform*.

The principles of neuro-science have been much popularised recently through Eric Jensen's The Learning Brain and Susan Greenfield's books, *The Human Brain: A Guided Tour, Brain Story,* and *The Private Life of the Brain*. This has influenced educational theory and led to the development of new ideas. Much of it can seem quite complex and difficult to apply to the classroom. However, Alastair Smith's *The Brain's Behind it* does a good job of de-mystifying the area.

Mind mapping

People seem to divide themselves into those who mind map and those who don't. The latter seem to think that the former need to mind map because 'normal' learning doesn't work for them. Then some 'mind mappers' apply a missionary zeal and think that all other forms of learning are nearly heretical.

The fundamental things about mind mapping are these:

- It can benefit everyone in certain situations at certain times
- It should work in tandem with – not to the exclusion of – other forms of working, eg timelines, basic notes, networked notes, etc
- If you have never attempted or practised the skill, then you have one less tool in the 'toolbag' when you need to try something different

Brain Gym

Of all the areas of accelerated learning that have attracted criticism Brain Gym is probably the most derided. The notion that physical actions can have an impact on the working of the brain seems far-fetched to many people and has been denounced as 'bad science'.

If you know your stuff and are not confusing 'energisers' with Brain Gym, then my advice is: *'if it works, use it and if it doesn't, don't'*. As a learner, I find that too much sitting typing at a screen makes me very tired and lethargic and that a few minutes of cross-lateral exercise can really bring me back to life.

Imagine that your body is divided in two by three lines (one splitting top and bottom, one left and right sides, and the final one separating front and back). Cross-lateral exercises force you to cross these centre lines and can include some activities that you may never have contemplated eg skipping, speed stacking, Thai boxing, juggling, knitting or even a bit of shuffling and jumpstyle!

Memory

Memory and memory skills have become quite the rock and roll of the intellect of late. Once the domain of stage acts, they have become a mainstay in schools and many people are intrigued by the characters involved in the World Memory Championships.

Those who take part in the championships are not fundamentally different from the rest of us, it is just that they have taken the basic principles of memory and practised them with an Olympian level of dedication – even referring to themselves as 'Mental Athletes'.

So, if we are all capable of having great memories and this is one of the routes to exam success, why don't more of us take up the flame and run?...

'Fixed' or 'growth' mindset?

... Largely because many of us subscribe to what Carol Dweck in *Mindset: the Psychology of Success* and Matthew Syed in *Bounce* refer to as the 'fixed mindset': the belief that intelligence and ability are innate (ie you are born with a skill set and it is fixed). This is in opposition to the 'growth mindset' (ie a belief that with the right training and coaching you are capable of great things even if you are just an 'average' person).

Possession of a 'growth mindset' has been found to be the single common factor among great sports people, who constantly reflect on their performance and look for areas to work on every time they fail – rather than putting disappointing results down to a lack of skill and, consequently, giving up.

10,000 hours

An important factor here is the concept of 10,000 hours of practice. This was first put forward in Malcolm Gladwell's book *Outliers* as being the amount of input required to reach the very top in any field. Matthew Syed in *Bounce* is keen to point out that those hours of practice must have an essential quality – that you continue to stretch yourself further. Running two miles every day at the same speed and intensity for the prescribed 10,000 hours will not get you to the Olympics.

Syed believes that our present school system has nearly institutionalised the fixed mindset and that if we are to defeat the demands of the 'satnav learner' we must find ways to incorporate into our teaching the ideas relating to a growth mindset.

It is also worth remembering that the people who put in 10,000 hours do it out of love and not as a response to coercion. Maybe if we follow the new edicts of Ofsted – to 'enthuse and engage' – then this will start to happen?

State

I mentioned initially three things that affect the teaching and learning process – **state**, **style** and **structure**. Historically, **state** (that is, the physical and emotional state of the learner) has been somewhat ignored on the basis that the teacher can do little to affect it.

Greater prominence has been given to the subject by Daniel Goleman's *Emotional Intelligence*. This amply demonstrates the importance of the 'EQ' (Emotional Quotient) factor, which is vital to students' true success in life. Developing this theme, Steve Bowkett's book *Self-intelligence, a Handbook for Developing Confidence, Self-esteem and Inter-personal Skills* is very user-friendly.

Until recently, much of the theory seemed to be developed in isolation from the rest of the curriculum and was only given importance at primary level with Guy Claxton's recent work (see *Building Learning Power*). He discusses four concepts: resilience, resourcefulness, reflectiveness and reciprocity. By helping our students to develop these qualities we are increasing their learning power.

The fifth stage of mastery...

Combining these ideas with advances in ICT and the development of coaching and mentoring in schools (see Mike Hughes *Coaching in Schools*), we are moving rapidly away from the notion that the teacher is the 'sage on the stage' to the idea of her being the 'guide from the side'.

We are also using the concept of 'scaffolding' to move learners through the four stages of learning:

- From the states of (i) unconscious or (ii) conscious incompetence
- Through (iii) conscious competence, to
- The state of (iv) unconscious competence and the new fifth stage of 'mastery'

The Big Picture

 Registering

 Retaining

 Recalling

 Healthy Mind

 Current Thinking

 Further Information ◀

Further Information

Brain dominance

The concept of hemispheric dominances first put forward in the late 1950s held that:

- The left hemisphere of the neo-cortex is responsible for all the logical, language-driven, sequential and detailed work
- The right hemisphere was its groovier partner responsible for the more holistic, image-driven, spontaneous and random work

Research has since shown the brain to be 'plastic' in its functioning. The idea that certain functions sit neatly in one half of the brain or the other is hard to justify. Neuroscience has shown that the whole brain is active all the time in everyone. (See *Learning & the Brain Pocketbook* for more about this.)

Interestingly, the creative industry is now recruiting 'diagonal thinkers', ie those who can come up with imaginative and novel ideas but then quickly see ways to implement them in a sequential, logical and detailed fashion.

www.achievementinmind.co.uk has some interesting material that builds on Carla Hannaford's concepts from '*The Dominance Factor*' – everything from individualised work plans to whole class work groups with a simple online test.

Intelligence types

It is said that after having had the concept of 'multiple intelligence' explained to him, an education minister replied that he 'simply didn't believe it'.

It is not necessary to be a believer to get the most out of this concept. The idea that intelligence could be neatly segmented into 7, 8, 10 or 14 types (the count keeps going up) is illogical. However, what the concept does give you is a structure for exploring the different realms that people might like to visit or the broad avenues they might like to travel down. It is often a better indication of your choice of hobby than job.

The eight basic types of intelligence can provide a great way to structure enrichment days, primary to secondary transition days and staff training days.

One school I have worked with over many years collapses its Year 9 timetable and has a day of students working in groups and visiting 'brain stations'. These require them to use their different styles of intelligence. The students and staff enjoy the day and all feel that they learn a lot. What they learn becomes part of a bigger, school-wide learning to learn programme.

Intelligence types

As a teacher, I always found the concept of multiple intelligences a great way of forcing variety into my lesson planning, especially incorporating intelligence types in which I am not strong. I once challenged myself to teach a lesson on glaciation using musical rhythmic ideas. It seemed that my lack of aptitude with all things rhythmic was the best part of the lesson!

I learned a lot, not just about my teaching but also about the students. When we extended the idea in an RE lesson to completing homework using any of the multiple intelligences, a student unexpectedly produced a demo tape of 'Life as a Sikh' to the tune of 'Oops, upside your head'! I still have the recording and can vividly remember the look of amazement on all the other students' faces when I played it to them – and the look of pleasure on his.

Intelligence types

The eight core intelligence types are generally agreed to be the following:
- Bodily/kinaesthetic (movement people)
- Verbal/linguistic (word people)
- Mathematical/logical (puzzle solvers)
- Musical/rhythmic (tonal people)
- Visual/spatial (perspective people)
- Inter-personal (people people!)
- Intra-personal (empathy people)
- Naturalistic (nature people)

The questionnaire at www.likemindslearning.co.uk will give you an idea of *your* intelligences.

To work with some of the ideas in these pages:
- Identify famous people who you think show a bias to each type of intelligence
- See how many jobs you can list, suiting each type of intelligence
- Think of different board games which might suit different styles of intelligence. (The jury is still out on whether Scrabble suits verbal linguistic or visual spatial intelligence!)

Books

Accelerated Learning (Teachers)
Learning to Learn – The Fourth Generation by G Claxton. TLO Ltd, 2006
Outstanding Lessons Pocketbook by C Bentley Davis. Teachers' Pocketbooks, 2011
The Teachers' Toolkit by P Ginnis. Crown House Publishing, 2002
Transforming Learning by S Norman. Saffire Press, 2003

Brain Gym and Brain Studies (Students and Teachers)
Brain Story by S Greenfield. BBC London, 2000
Learning & The Brain Pocketbook by E Dommet et al. Teachers' Pocketbooks, 2010
Smart Moves by C Hannaford. Great Ocean Publishers, 1995.
The Brain's Behind it by A Smith. Network Educational Press Ltd, 2004
The Dominance Factor by C Hannaford. Great Ocean Publishers, 1997
The Human Brain: A Guided Tour by S Greenfield. Weidenfeld and Nicolson, 1997
The Private Life of the Brain by S Greenfield. Penguin, 2000

Emotional Intelligence (Students and Teachers)
Authentic Happiness: Using the New Positive Psychology to Realize Your Potential for Lasting Fulfillment by M Seligman. Free Press, 2003
Beating Anger: The eight point plan for coping with rage by M Fisher. Rider, 2005
Human Givens by J Griffin & I Tyrrell. HG Publishing, 2004

Books

Learned Optimism M Seligman. Free Press, 1998
The Mind Gym by The Mind Gym. Time Warner Books, 2005

Learning Power (Teachers)
Building Learning Power by G Claxton. TLO Ltd, 2002
Mindset: the New Psychology of Success by C Dweck. Random House, 2006
Outliers the Story of Success by M Gladwell. Allen Lane, 2008
The Power of Diversity by B Prashnig. Network Educational Press Ltd, 2004
Tweak to Transform by M Hughes & D Potter. Network Educational Press Ltd, 2002

Motivation (Students and Teachers)
Bounce: The myth of talent and the power of practice by M Syed. Fourth Estate, 2011
The Element: How Finding Your Passion Changes Everything by K Robinson and L
Aronica. Penguin Books, 2009
The Luck Factor by R Wiseman. Century Publishing, 2003
Why do I need a teacher when I've got Google? by I Gilbert. Routledge Press, 2011

Revising (Students)
How to Pass Exams: Accelerate Your Learning, Memorise Key Facts, Revise Effectively
by D O'Brien. Hodder Headline, 2003

About the author

Tom Barwood

Tom has always had one simple goal in life – to be an inspiration. As a classroom teacher he developed a rapport and teaching style that brought that goal to life. Excited by developments in brain-based learning, he became a freelance trainer and is now director and main course-provider of Likeminds Consulting.

Since 2001 Tom has visited hundreds of schools in Britain, mainland Europe and the Middle East, ranging from prestigious independent schools to state schools and academies in the most challenging areas. He has worked with pupils across the age and ability range and with Secondary and Primary teachers from NQTs to headteachers, and in groups from 5 to 500.

Tom specialises in all aspects of teaching and learning but has achieved prominence for his work on stretching the more able and maximising boys' potential. He has trained as a schools inspector and is a chair of governors. However, it is Tom's innate enthusiasm, passion for learning and unswerving commitment to creativity in the classroom that mark him out as different. Tom can be contacted directly through www.likemindslearning.co.uk